FURTHER FABULOUS CANADIANS!

Hysterically Historical Rhymes

*To dear Gordon and Mort –
Hope you enjoy this new
gallery of Canadians!
with love from*

GORDON SNELL

Gordon Snell

with caricatures by

AISLIN

McArthur & Company
Toronto

December 2004

Published in Canada in 2004 by
McArthur & Company
322 King St. West, Suite 402, Toronto, Ontario M5V 1J2
www.mcarthur-co.com

Library and Archives Canada Cataloguing in Publication

Snell, Gordon
Further fabulous Canadians! :
hysterically historical rhymes / Gordon
Snell ; with caricatures by Aislin.

ISBN 1-55278-445-2

1. Celebrities--Canada--Poetry. 2. Humorous poetry, English.
3. Canadian wit and humor, Pictorial. I. Aislin II. Title.

PR6069.N44F87 2004   821'.914   C2004-904242-4

Cover Illustration by *AISLIN*
Layout, Design, and Electronic Imaging by *MARY HUGHSON*
Printed and Bound in Canada by
Friesens Corporation

The publisher would like to acknowledge the financial support of the
Government of Canada through the Book Publishing Industry
Development Program, the Canada Council for the Arts, and the
Ontario Arts Council for our publishing activities. We also acknowl-
edge the Government of Ontario through the Ontario Media
Development Corporation Ontario Book Initiative.

10 9 8 7 6 5 4 3 2

McArthur & Company
Toronto

Canadians from many ages
Parade in triumph through our pages.
These rhymes in which they're celebrated
To Maeve, with love, are dedicated.

GS

This book is dedicated to Two-Votes
To that special beach in Mexico,
And all the other beaches
We have yet to discover.
A

FURTHER FABULOUS CANADIANS!

Hysterically Historical Rhymes

Contents

THE CANADA GOOSE
(*Branta Canadensis*)

*(Canada Geese with their distinctive honking cry
make a majestic sight as they fly in huge numbers through the sky.
But not everyone admires them: some regard them as
a messy nuisance and a threat, and seek to cull them,
while they also face danger from the guns of the hunter.)*

HONK, HONK!
Now let the heavens ring –
The Canada Geese are on the wing.
Behold us, making our migrations
In V for Victory formations.
HONK, HONK!
We voice our cry melodious –
Why do some humans find it odious?

BANG, BANG!
Cracks out the hunter's gun –
They want to kill us, just for fun,
And justify their cruel ballistics
With very dubious statistics.
BANG, BANG!
Our ways they may condemn –
But have we done more harm than them?

HONK, HONK!
My goslings, warmly nuzzling,
You'll find the world a little puzzling.
You'll grow up beautiful and proud
Then hear that sound so fierce and loud,
BANG, BANG!
Your life is soon cut short:
The human species call it sport.

HONK, HONK!
Like loons and beavers too
We are Canadians through and through –
And carrying our nation's name,
We fly with it to world-wide fame.
HONK, HONK!
Let Man come to his senses –
Befriending *Branta Canadensis*.

MARTIN FROBISHER
(1539 – 1594)

*(Martin Frobisher was a hot-tempered pirate chief who became
one of the explorers sent to find the North West Passage through
the Canadian Arctic to China and the Far East. His discoveries on
Baffin Island, near the bay he named after himself, led to
a fever of speculation and further adventurous voyages.)*

Now here's to Martin Frobisher
A pirate bold was he
And in the wake of Francis Drake
He sailed the foaming sea.

He wore no skull and crossbones
And all that pirate stuff,
But silken breeches, fancy stitches
And a smart white ruff.

He was hired to go exploring
And with three little ships
Set forth towards the frozen north –
The first of several trips.

Now Queen Elizabeth, no less,
On Martin did rely

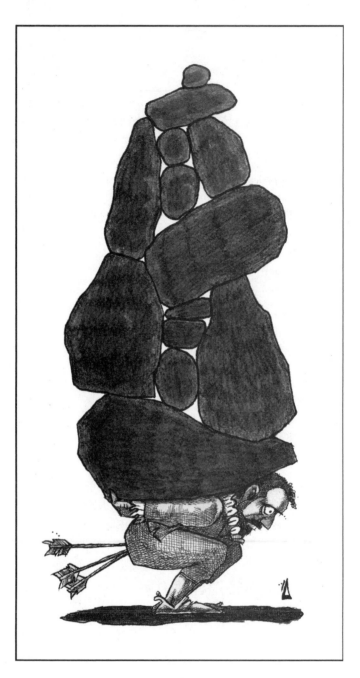

And as he sailed, that Good Queen Bess
Came out to wave goodbye.

The North West Passage was their quest
And the riches of Cathay.
In Frobisher Bay they came to rest
And said: "We're on our way."

"America is on our left
And Asia on our right."
So on they sailed, but found they'd failed:
A dead end came in sight.

They thought they saw some porpoises
As slowly they did cruise –
But closer to, they had a view
Of Inuit in canoes.

Five sailors went ashore with them,
To look at the terrain.
Dead or alive, those sailors five
Were never seen again.

An Inuit, captured in revenge,
Was brought across the ocean,
But stones they'd found upon the ground
Caused even more commotion.

They had the black stone analysed
As Martin watched and smiled.
"There's gold inside!" one expert cried,
And everyone went wild.

The Queen again backed Frobisher,
For riches were in store
So off went he across the sea
To dig that distant shore.

With Inuit there were skirmishes:
Their aim was far superior,
And Martin got some arrows shot
Right into his posterior.

He took two hundred tons of rock,
And Inuit captives too;
And though back home some chose to mock,
The gold-rush fever grew.

A third trip brought back even more,
But Martin's face did fall
When smelting showed that all that ore
Contained no gold at all.

He sighed and said: "Disgrace for me
Has left my backers flat.
I'll just go back to piracy –
At least I'm good at that!"

When Spain with its Armada came
To fight the English fleet
Then Martin once more made his name
And helped in Spain's defeat.

He was made Sir Martin Frobisher –
He'd had both fame and slander;
Though not one jot of gold he got,
He was Master and Commander.

SIEUR D'IBERVILLE
(1661 – 1706)

(Canadian-born Sieur d'Iberville was one of the military leaders whose many raids and battles by land and sea established the colonies of New France. In the late 17th and early 18th century these stretched from Hudson Bay south as far as the Mississippi Delta.)

When they settled in New France
Men of spirit got a chance
Their fame and fortune to advance.

One such was Charles le Moyne, who'd been
Brought here from France aged just fifteen,
A servant of the Jesuits;
With enterprise he used his wits
In trade and commerce, and he planned
Some profitable deals in land.
Among the rich in Montreal
He was the wealthiest of all.

Of his eleven sons, Pierre
In fierce forays would do and dare
To fight wherever it persists
The power of English colonists.

Pierre and his big brother Jacques
Led the Canadiens to attack
The village of Schenectady,
And there with ruthless savagery
They quite subdued the population,
Thanks largely to assassination.

Five times he led into the fray
A fighting force in Hudson Bay.
The English saw their first fort fall
When Pierre himself had scaled the wall;
Then d'Iberville and Jacques his brother
Saw one fort fall and then another.
With all the English chased away,
Sieur d'Iberville and France held sway
Over the whole of Hudson Bay.

Audaciously Pierre now planned
A fierce attack in Newfoundland.
He'd launch his daring raids upon
The stretch of land called Avalon.

From west to east his force would go
Across the wastes of ice and snow.
No other force from shore to shore
Had dared to go that way before.
Pierre's solution, though, was neat:
His men put snowshoes on their feet.

They travelled thus with some velocity
And then attacked with great ferocity.
The soldiers of Sieur d'Iberville
Two hundred settlers did kill,
And Pierre no doubt was overjoyed
To see a hundred boats destroyed.

"Angel of Wrath" the British called him –
We do not think the term appalled him.
As trophies of this grim attack
A load of scalps was soon sent back
To show to Governor Frontenac.

For all his furious rampages,
Pierre was certainly courageous.
He planned to take York Factory fort
But in thick fog he got caught short.
Sieur d'Iberville did not delay –
He sailed on into Hudson Bay,
Believing, though the light was dim,
His ships would soon catch up with him.

Then sure enough, the fog did clear
And soon he saw three masts appear.
Before a greeting left his lips
He realized they were English ships!

Their guns, when all was said and done,
Outnumbered his by three to one.
Although he was the lone defender
Sieur d'Iberville would not surrender.

He sailed towards his foes instead,
Guns blazing and full speed ahead.
The frigate fired – a cannon ball
Toppled his rigging, sails and all;
But firing promptly back at it,
He scored a devastating hit.

Two ships closed in – Pierre had seen them
And with a zig-zag sailed between them.
He could have fled and got away
And sailed out into Hudson Bay,
But then his foes he did astound:
Instead of fleeing, he turned around.

Once more an all-out war he waged –
For four fierce hours the battle raged
Until the frigate, out of luck,
Below the waterline was struck.

It quickly sank beneath the waves,
Taking the crew to watery graves.
Two other ships were lurking there
And one surrendered to Pierre.

The other, tiring of the fight,
Across the bay was taking flight.

His own ship sank – the crew survived;
And then at last the fleet arrived.
Pierre his plan would not forsake:
The fort he soon went on to take.

King Louis d'Iberville would thank
By giving him Chevalier rank
And saying: "Your style's so fast and nippy –
Run down and take the Mississippi!
And then extend our panorama
And take control of Alabama."

Now France's colonies held sway
From the Deep South to Hudson Bay –
A situation, many feel,
Helped hugely by Sieur d'Iberville.

Writers about him often feel
That "swashbuckling" was his appeal –
And when life put him to the test,
He swashed his buckle with the best.

GEORGE TOWNSHEND
(1724 – 1807)

*(George Townshend came from an aristocratic family
and joined the army as a young man. He was one of the three
Brigadiers under General James Wolfe's command during
the battle for Quebec in 1759. A talented artist, he drew
caricatures of anyone he disliked in public or private life.)*

In English eyes, George Townshend had
What really makes a guy count:
He was a wealthy, well-born lad
And Daddy was a Viscount!

So Wolfe, when Townshend joined his band,
Was not inclined to love him:
He felt that George was much too grand
And thought himself above him.

The General was a moody man
And somehow he'd arrange it
That every time he made a plan
He'd promptly go and change it.

The walls took quite a battering
While Wolfe planned his attack;
The Brigadiers were chattering
Behind their General's back.

While he was dithering about,
Oblivious to their strictures,
George got his pen and paper out
And started drawing pictures.

His fierce and expert artistry
Was savage and perfidious:
He made the General out to be
Deformed and crass and hideous.

His colleagues found the cartoons fun –
With laughter they were pealing;
But when the General spotted one
He nearly hit the ceiling.

The pair then had a raging row,
But George thought: "What the heck?
He can't do much about it now –
It's time to storm Quebec!"

The bullets flew, and on the ground
The stricken Wolfe lay bleeding –
And when he died, George Townshend found
That he himself was leading!

The French had battled for New France
And in the end had failed.
Now, when George Townshend got the chance,
For home he quickly sailed.

For fame and triumph George might thirst,
But he would surely soonest
Be honoured as the very first
Canadian cartoonist!

THOMAS D'ARCY McGEE
(1825 – 1868)

(Born in Ireland, Thomas D'Arcy McGee came to Montreal
in 1857 after an active career in revolutionary politics and
journalism in the U.S.A. and at home. He was elected to Canada's
assembly in 1858 and later joined up with Prime Minister
John A Macdonald. A passionate believer in unity for the North
American Colonies, he became one of the Fathers of Confederation.)

(These verses match the tune of the old Irish ballad,
'The Wild Colonial Boy.')

There was a Wild Colonial Boy,
His name it was McGee.
He was born and raised in Ireland,
And he crossed the foaming sea.
His temper raged just like the waves,
And some did not enjoy
The fiery fight for justice of
The Wild Colonial Boy.

In Ireland and the U.S.A. a rebel he became,
And yet it was in Canada
He rose to greatest fame.
He spoke up for the Catholics
In brave and ringing tones

And Protestants would hurl abuse,
As well as sticks and stones.

He got a seat in Parliament,
His oratory was strong:
He said the colonies should all
To one great land belong.
He teamed up with Macdonald
In the House and at the bar,
And drunken ramblings now and then,
Their eloquence would mar.

The Cabinet administered a gentle reprimand;
Macdonald nodded gravely
And declared: "I understand.
Two drunkards in the Cabinet's
Too many, I admit –
And I am telling you, McGee,
That I ain't going to quit!"

But when McGee was sober,
His powerful words would flow.
He said Confederation was the only way to go:
"Canadian nationality will fill us all with joy –
We'll be colonies no longer," said
The Wild Colonial Boy.

At Charlottetown and in Quebec
And then in London town,
McGee was there to talk, persuade,
And calm the doubters down.
So of Confederation, a Father he became –
And then a big debate began
About the nation's name.

Some wanted Aquilonia, and some Victorialand,
While others said Superior
Would make us all feel grand.
Hochelaga featured too – on all,
McGee poured scorn:
"Imagine having to declare:
'I'm Hochelagander born!'"

So Canada became the name –
What helped the land unite
Were Fenians on the border,
Preparing for a fight.
McGee condemned them savagely
With every fiery breath,
Which earned him many praises,
And many threats of death.

McGee achieved election
And he helped to legislate

In Ottawa, for people of the newest nation-state,
Until, one still and moonlit night,
Near his lodgings in the town
By a lone assassin's bullet
He was suddenly cut down.

As shock and fear convulsed the land,
The Fenians were blamed,
And firm Canadian unity
Against them was proclaimed.
Now among the nation's founders,
Lasting fame he does enjoy:
The first Canadian martyr was
The Wild Colonial Boy.

SARAH EMMA EDMONDS
(1841 – 1898)

*(As a young girl Sarah Emma Edmonds left home to escape
her father, disguised herself as a young man, and joined
the Union army in the American Civil War. She had a colourful
career as a spy before she returned to civilian life, became a wife
and mother and wrote a best-selling book about her life.)*

Sarah Emma Edmonds was a master of disguise
She learned it at a very early age.
Her father was a tyrant, so it's really no surprise
That in her teens she left home in a rage.

In New Brunswick then
She opened up a shop for ladies' hats
And soon a novel new career began;
But if her father found her
He would go completely bats
So she thought she would pretend to be a man.

She became young Franklin Thompson
And very soon was hired:
As a salesman selling Bibles she was travelling.

Soon at company headquarters
Her skills were much admired:
Her deception showed no danger
Of unravelling.

When the U.S. Civil War began in 1861,
In Michigan she joined up as a private.
She fought in several combats
Like the Battle of Bull Run
And soldiering she really seemed to thrive at.

Seeking even more adventures,
She joined the secret service –
In the face of any danger she'd be brave.
Her first mission as a spy
Didn't even make her nervous
When she blacked her face
And dressed up as a slave.

And so with the Confederates
She lived inside a fort –
The first of many such successful missions:
With her inside information
She was able to report
On the opposition's guns and troop positions.

She posed then as a female slave
And as a merchant's clerk

And as an Irish peddler cut a dash.
With style and dedication
She performed her secret work –
She could rival 007 for panache!

Her spy career was ended
When malaria laid her low –
Now she could pose no longer as a boy.
She switched to her own gender
And was able then to go
To a hospital in Cairo, Illinois.

When she was cured and ready
To rejoin the army scene
There came a piece of news that truly hurt her:
Private Franklin Thompson
By his regiment had been
Officially declared as a deserter.

She married a New Brunswick man,
A carpenter by trade,
Had children then, and wrote her story too;
And later she decided
It was time she should be paid
The veteran's army pension she was due.

She got her way when regimental comrades
Took her side:
She had played a major role
In both the sexes,
And Sarah Emma Edmonds
Was buried when she died
Among the veterans' graves
In Houston, Texas.

WILLIAM LYON MACKENZIE KING
(1874 – 1950)

(King was the grandson of the 1837 rebel leader,
William Lyon Mackenzie, but had a much more cautious
personality. First elected as a Liberal to the House of Commons
in 1908, he became Canada's longest reigning Prime Minister,
winning six elections and pursuing sometimes contradictory
policies. He led a united Canada through the Second World War
and the boom years that followed it.)

William Lyon Mackenzie King
Clung to his mother's apron string –
And his Mamma was far from critical
When William chose to get political:
If politics absorbed his life
He really didn't need a wife!

In Parliament he made his name –
The Liberals' leader he became.
King, welcomed with admiring cheers,
Led them for nearly thirty years.

Into the fray he boldly bounced –
Meighen's Conservatives were trounced.

For years King led a coalition
While Meighen fumed in opposition.

Then King's support began to waver;
A bold solution he would favour:
The Governor General, he'd declare,
Should call elections then and there.
"I won't!" Lord Byng, the G.G., said.
"Meighen shall govern in your stead."

Three days of power Meighen tasted;
The Governor General was lambasted
By furious Mackenzie King:
"A devious meddler, that's Lord Byng!
He's trying to play colonial tricks
With our Canadian politics!"

Whether King's view was right or wrong,
Most of the voters went along:
The Governor General, they said,
Should henceforth be a figurehead.
Though Byng might grumble, grouse and glower,
Mackenzie King was back in power.

And now he started to create
The groundwork for a welfare state.
(Not for First Nations – they would note
Their chance of justice was remote:
They didn't even get to vote.)

King's style was full of incongruity –
He liked strategic ambiguity.
Elusive, cunning, enigmatic,
And brilliantly bureaucratic,
He seemed to move, while staying static.

In séances he sometimes tried
Communing with The Other Side,
And asked dead leaders if they knew
What policies he should pursue;
He tried to reach his mother, too.

King joined the War, but said: "It's clear
We're having no conscription here."
Instead, he sent each volunteer
Who'd signed up for defence alone
Abroad into the battle zone.

Conscription came – though many grieved
That somehow they had been deceived.
Mackenzie King just dodged and weaved,
And got his moral stance believed.

At home, his policies were hard:
Most Jewish refugees were barred,
And Japanese Canadians found
For "relocation" they were bound.

King made such harsh rules with impunity,
And still maintained Canadian unity.
After the war, he let the nation
Reluctantly, take immigration,
But made the rules as he thought right,
To favour those whose skin was white.

And yet, King helped to lay foundations
That started the United Nations,
And turned, with diplomatic stealth,
An Empire to a Commonwealth.

His final stature's still a mystery –
Perhaps the verdict of our history
Will always have a lingering doubt:
Years later, still the jury's out.

Just as he sought for a result
By dabbling with things occult,
Perhaps in rooms discreet and dim
Our leaders are consulting him!

DR. MAHLON LOCKE
(1880 – 1951)

(Born on a farm near Williamsburg, Ontario, Mahlon Locke
became a brilliant medical student at Queen's University.
He went on to do postgraduate work at Edinburgh in Scotland,
where he learned the techniques of foot manipulation. As a doctor
back in Williamsburg, his methods had such success that
eventually he was treating thousands of patients a day.)

Doctor Locke said: "In my practice
With patients, I can tell,
If they're rheumatic, then the fact is
Their feet are flat as well."

"I'll try a treatment swift and neat
And put it to the test:
Once I have fixed the patient's feet,
Let Nature do the rest."

A local blacksmith came to him
With fierce rheumatic pain.
He said: "The future's looking grim –
I'll never work again!"

The doctor moved his feet around
And soon the pain receded.

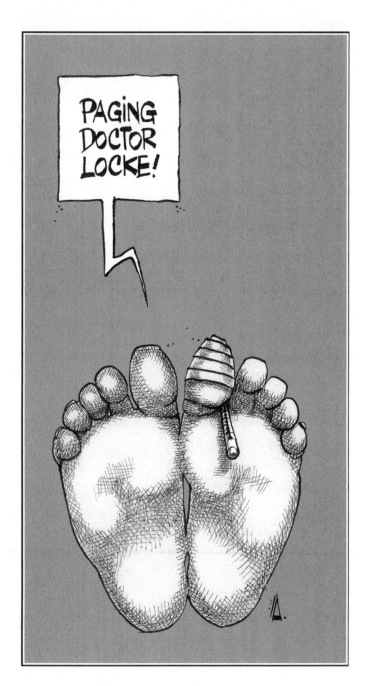

Amazed, the grateful blacksmith found
The treatment had succeeded.

With leather inserts in each shoe
To keep his arches raised,
The blacksmith said: "I'm good as new –
Let Doctor Locke be praised!"

And soon the blacksmith spread the word
And other patients came.
Years passed, and a reporter heard
About the doctor's claim.

He said: "I've got arthritis, Doc,
It pains me through and through."
"Show me your feet," said Doctor Locke,
"I'll see what I can do."

When the arthritis went away
The journalist, amazed,
Said: "Now throughout the U.S.A.
In papers you'll be praised."

In print and on the radio
Reports came loud and lyrical.
This doctor in Ontario
They said, could work a miracle.

Soon people came from many lands
In buses, boats and trains
So Doctor Locke with magic hands
Could cure their aches and pains.

In Morrisburg, not far away,
An ocean liner moored
Where well-heeled patients came to stay
While waiting to be cured.

But Doctor Locke cared nothing for
His patients' wealth or station.
He charged a dollar and no more
For each manipulation.

Princes and paupers came, and so
Did Mrs Roosevelt.
They all queued up there, row on row,
To have their arches felt.

In time his skill and speed increased –
Such was his pace and power
That he was treating at the least
Two hundred every hour.

The Mayo Clinic wanted him
But Doctor Locke said: "No,
In Williamsburg I'll sink or swim –
Here I can run the show."

Though testimonials galore
And praise he did not lack,
Some doctors, envious to the core,
Declared he was a quack.

But Doctor Locke just didn't care –
His treatment was no con;
Though he became a millionaire,
He simply carried on.

No critics now could dent his fame
Though they might do their worst.
To Doctor Locke the crowds still came,
Whose motto was FEET FIRST!

LAWREN HARRIS
(1885 – 1970)

*(Born in Brantford, Ontario, where his family's Massey-Harris
Company was based, Lawren Harris studied art in Toronto
and Berlin before becoming an artillery officer in World War One.
He returned to Canada and was one of the founders of
the Group of Seven, the artists who chose the wilderness landscapes
of Canada as their subject, and whose controversial exhibitions
revolutionized Canadian art.)*

Before the Group of Seven came,
Canadian art was rather tame:
Portraits and pastures, grazing cows,
Little excitement could arouse.

Although the paintings were sedate
The frames were splendidly ornate.
Their owners' pleasure was intensive:
The pictures all looked so expensive.

Young painters came along, whose art
Would soon upset the applecart.
Tom Thomson was among the first –
Upon the art scene he would burst

With rugged landscapes setting forth
The wildest splendours of the North.

Lawren Harris was his friend –
Together they would go and spend
With other artists, many weeks
Camping among the lakes and peaks,
Sketching and painting what they saw –
A land magnificent and raw.

Now Harris was that creature rare:
An artist who had cash to spare.
He numbered in his family tree
The Massey-Harris Company.

A studio building was erected
Where struggling artists he selected
Could have a place to come and paint.
Tom Thomson said; "My style that ain't!
Really, for me it's much too grand."
Lawren said: "Tom, I understand.
We'll fit you out a little shack
Just like a cabin, at the back."

Though four years later, Thomson drowned,
His influence was still profound:
So seven painters of like mind
In one campaigning group combined.
To jolt the art world was their mission

With their first startling exhibition.
And so in those Toronto halls
Their paintings glowed upon the walls
With brush-strokes bold and colours blazing
In scenes where not one cow was grazing,
But clouds came tumbling down the skies
And stark and jagged trees did rise
Against the snow and ancient stone
Of lands uncharted and unknown.

Such pictures, rarely seen before,
Caused instantly a great furor,
And these artistic pioneers
Were greeted with abuse and sneers.
For epithets the critics forage:

One said: "They're like hot mush or porridge!"
Another critic found a new lash:
"They should be called Hungarian Goulash!"

Not everyone was thinking so:
Debate was raging to and fro
And Lawren Harris said: "The fighting
Is all great fun, and quite exciting.
Canadian Art, in all this strife,
At least is showing signs of life!"

Soon other critics had their say
In England and the U.S.A.:

Triumphant praises came their way,
And now the Group had come to stay.

At home, the old tradition's faction
Went on to fight a rearguard action;
But more shows marked the Group's success
And left the critics in distress.
Soon they'd expand, and found with pride
A group of painters, nation-wide.

Now Lawren Harris would impart
More abstract features to his art:
Majestic icebergs, lakes of white,
And frozen peaks that tower in height.

He looked back on what he believed
The Group of Seven had achieved:
They set Canadian artists free
To paint the noble land they see.
Their art would be, for their own nation,
An endless act of re-creation.

TOM THREE PERSONS
(1888 – 1949)

*(Tom Three Persons grew up on the Blood Reserve
in southern Alberta, where he learned the horseman's skills
he used in cattle roundups and rodeos. At one time he had
his own herds, but it was his talent as a cowboy which gave him
his greatest triumph at the bronco-riding contest in 1912
at the first Calgary Stampede.)*

Tom Three Persons was a cowboy
Of a very special breed.
He went riding into legend
At the Calgary Stampede.

On the Blood Reserve he grew up –
There his riding skills he'd test;
At the local ranchers' roundups
Tom was rated with the best.

Now at fairs and at rodeos
Tom Three Persons would compete;
At the art of bronco-busting
He was very hard to beat.

Then Alberta's cattle barons
Thought they'd stage a rodeo:
It would be the Best and Biggest
Grandest, Greatest Wild West Show.

Big parades and exhibitions
Crowds of thousands did enthral,
But the bronco-busting contest
Was the greatest thrill of all.

Cowboys came there by the hundred
To Alberta's rodeo
From the distant U.S. prairies
And the plains of Mexico.

When they made the draw for horses
Tom Three Persons' smile was grim,
For the dreaded bronc called Cyclone
Would be saddled up for him.

Snarling Cyclone stood there stamping,
With his coat all glossy black;
In his time, three hundred cowboys
Had been flung from off his back.

Still they came to try to tame him –
All of them would face defeat
When his back went into action
Like a plane's ejection seat.

Tom was now the last contestant –
There could be no thought of truce
When he leaped into the saddle
And he shouted: "Let him loose!"

Cyclone fiercely lunged and twisted,
Cyclone raced across the field.
Cyclone bucked and lurched and snorted –
Tom Three Persons would not yield.

Then the horse reared on his hind-legs
Like some crazy circus act.
Up and up his hooves reached skyward,
But his rider stayed intact.

How the joyful crowds were cheering,
Urging Tom Three Persons on.
Every moment now expecting
They would see the rider gone.

Each time Cyclone reared, Tom bellowed
With a fierce and furious sound,
Till at last the horse, exhausted,
Stayed with four feet on the ground.

Would he buck again, they wondered,
Pitching Tom into the air?
But he simply stood there panting,
With a grim, defeated glare.

Then around the field they galloped,
Cyclone docile as a child –
Other horsemen galloped with them
– While the roaring crowd went wild.

Honours showered on Tom Three Persons
Who subdued that fiercesome steed
And went riding into legend
At the Calgary Stampede.

COUGAR ANNIE
(1888 – 1985)

*(In 1915, Ada Annie Rae-Arthur with her husband and children
came from Vancouver to settle on a five-acre tract of forest
wilderness at Boat on the west coast of Vancouver Island.
With great hardship, they cleared the land and made a nursery
garden with livestock and a general store. Defending her land
against prowling animals, Annie used her shotgun skills so well
that she earned the nickname 'Cougar Annie'. After four husbands
and eleven children, she finally left her home and beloved garden
when she was over ninety. Cougar Annie's garden became derelict
but was lovingly restored by Peter Buckland and is now run
as a tourist attraction and botanical study centre by
the Boat Basin Foundation.)*

They called her Cougar Annie,
And she well deserved the name,
As she strolled around, a shotgun in her hand.
With a husband and three children
To the wilderness she came
To try to hack a living from the land.

With crosscut saws and axes
They began to fell the trees –
It could sometimes take a day
To saw one through.

And once the tree had fallen,
They were nearly on their knees,
But they somehow had to get the stump out too.

Some blasted them with gunpowder,
Some levered them with poles –
The tree stumps were as tough as any boulder.
Cougar Annie would set fire to them,
And like a pile of coals,
In the ground for several weeks
They'd glow and smoulder.

They used the fallen trees
To build a homestead and some sheds –
They kept chickens, geese and ducks,
And goats as well,
While Annie planned a garden
And she dug out many beds
For vegetables and flowers that she could sell.

They somehow made a living,
And had eight more children too,
So it was very hard to make ends meet.
They later recollected that as the family grew
Sometimes porridge was the only thing to eat.

They opened up a general store
Where groceries were sold,

Among them cans whose labels said:
'Boiled Dinner'.
She got a name for selling eggs
She kept till they were old,
And bad and ancient eggs were not a winner.

But Annie's garden flourished
And exotic flowers were there –
She knew the Latin name of every one.
The livestock could be threatened
By a cougar or a bear,
But they met their match
When Annie got her gun.

She laid traps overnight
To catch the creatures by their paws
And next day dispatched
Them with a single shot.
The skins were very valuable,
And then the bounty laws
Meant quite a sum of money could be got.

Out in the bay, her husband drowned –
Though Cougar Annie grieved
She knew she couldn't manage by herself.
With a newspaper advertisement,
She fervently believed
She wouldn't long be left upon the shelf.

"Partner sought by BC widow,"
The advertisement averred,
"With a nursery and orchard to her name."
It added that a widower
Would really be preferred,
And that matrimony also was the aim.

George Campbell came along then,
Her husband's place to take –
A man of sixty, very far from gentle.
One day he cleaned his shotgun
And it went off by mistake,
Though rumours said it wasn't accidental.

More advertisements, more husbands –
There were four of them all told,
And another man there now and then would be.
Cougar Annie stuck it out there till,
Growing blind and old,
She left when she was over ninety-three.

When she died, her glorious garden
Grew forlorn and overgrown,
But now restored, it flourishes again.
Perhaps her joyful spirit comes
To wander there alone
And sings a most appropriate refrain:

"I don't need a Luger
To slay that snarling cougar
My shotgun will score in one.
And husbands a-plenty
I've had since I was twenty –
Yes, You Can Get A Man With A Gun!"

SAMUEL BRONFMAN
(1889 – 1971)

*(Samuel Bronfman was born on board ship while his parents were
emigrating from Russia to Canada. In Saskatchewan and
Manitoba, the family lived on his father's various jobs as a
salesman, horse-trader and hotel manager, until they started in the
liquor business. His son, "Mister Sam", had shrewd business
talents and the instinct for a good deal, and the huge market for
liquor during Prohibition days started him off on the building of
a world-wide and still flourishing empire.)*

*(These verses match the tune of the old folk-song,
'Nancy Whisky', also known as 'The Calton Weaver.')*

Out from Russia the Bronfmans travelled
To Canadian shores they came.
Though Sam was born in mid-Atlantic,
Water didn't make his name!

    Whisky, whisky, Bronfman's whisky,
    Whisky, whisky, from Mister Sam.

Sam watched his father trading horses,
Then adjourning to the bar.
Sam said: "Let's sell drink, not horses
That is where the profits are!"

So they started a liquor business,
In Yorkton first, then Montreal;
But the anti-drink campaigners
For Prohibition began to call.

    Whisky, whisky, they hate that whisky,
    Whisky, whisky they want to ban.

But Sam Bronfman he keeps on blending,
Those do-gooders they cast no gloom.
Alcohol is allowed for medicine –
How the sales of medicines boom!

Then by U.S. legislators
Harsher liquor laws are made.
Across the lakes, across the border,
Mister Sam did a roaring trade.

    Whisky, whisky, bootleg whisky,
    Whisky, whisky from Mister Sam.

Sam he bought an old distillery
Up for sale in Ontario,
And it went by the name of Seagram,
A name the world would come to know.

With liquor legal, Sam built his empire,
Chivas flourished, and so did Crown.

Samuel Bronfman made a fortune
From the drinkers who gulped them down.

Whisky, whisky, they loved his whisky,
Whisky, whisky from Mister Sam!

DR. NORMAN BETHUNE
(1890 – 1939)

*(Norman Bethune was born in Gravenhurst, Ontario, where his
family home is now kept as a memorial museum. He was wounded
in the First World War, then completed his medical studies and
became a surgeon. He was unconventional and inventive, and
believed passionately in medicine for all. His socialist outlook
led him to go to the battlefront in the Spanish Civil War, and later
to join Mao Tse-tung's army in China.)*

Norman Bethune began his life
Son of a minister and his wife,
And their religion, they'd insist,
Was fervently evangelist.

Perhaps this background made him feel
An almost missionary zeal.
His mission was to cure and heal,
And he pursued this strong vocation
With life-long, fiery dedication.

After his war-time service, he
A surgeon would set out to be.
He married, travelled, settled down
At a big hospital in town:

There in Detroit, his fate looked grim –
Tuberculosis came to him.

During his treatment he suggested
That an experiment be tested:
There was a surgical technique
Which TB sufferers could seek.
The chest was opened, and in there
The surgeon started blowing air.

So Norman asked the powers-that-be:
"Why don't you try this out on me?"
Reluctantly, the staff agreed;
He was convinced they would succeed.
In two months he was re-assured –
He found himself completely cured.

In Montreal he worked for years
As one of surgery's pioneers.
He did research, and for a spell
Invented instruments as well.
His style was thought unorthodox
And gave his colleagues several shocks.

Now Dr. Archibald, his boss,
Became at times extremely cross.
"Norman," he said, "it seems your creed
Is doing surgery at speed.

You take risks, and I'd even claim
That breaking records is your aim!"

Norman Bethune did not admire
The usual medical attire.
He said: "My colleagues, I confess,
Resemble in their way of dress
A cross between, in their tradition,
A Maitre d' and a mortician."

But he was seriously concerned
In medicine, that the poor were spurned.
Campaigning fiercely, he advised
That medicine should be socialized.

Then he was asked to lead a corps
And join the Spanish Civil War.
In Spain, much thanks and great esteem
Greeted his blood transfusion team.
In the front line, in mire and mud,
He gave the wounded soldiers blood.

This hard and dangerous work had tired him,
But then another cause inspired him:
In 1937 began
China's invasion by Japan.
Though some might think his plan was barmy,
He joined with Mao Tse-tung's Red Army.

There with the front-line troops once more
He battled through the trials of war,
Trained doctors there, and nurses too,
And operated all night through.
A finger-cut became infected
And septicaemia was suspected.
Though every remedy was tried,
There in the midst of war, he died.
A Chinese hero he became:
A hospital now bears his name.
A new stamp and a monument
Are part too of his testament.

And Chairman Mao Tse-tung, no less,
Paid tribute to his selflessness.
For such great deeds his name will stand
At home, and in that far-off land.

SIR FREDERICK BANTING
(1891 – 1941)

*(Born in Alliston, Ontario, Frederick Banting served in the Army
Medical Corps during the first World War, and then tried
unsuccessfully to establish a practice in London, Ontario. While
there he had an idea of a way to treat the then killer disease of
diabetes. He went to Toronto and was taken on by Professor J.J.R.
Macleod, and with him and two other scientists, Charles Best and
Dr. J.B. Collip, developed the extract called insulin which continues
to save the lives of countless diabetes sufferers all over the world.)*

Now diabetics everywhere
Their praises should be granting
To one who eased their dread disease:
His name was Frederick Banting.

In London in Ontario
He glumly said: "The fact is,
No patients come – I must be dumb
To try and run a practice!"

But one night when he tossed and turned
In sleepless desperation,
Into his mind there came a blinding
Flash of inspiration.

He jotted down some scribbled lines –
It was no thorough treatise –
But he was sure he'd found a cure
To deal with diabetes.

He cried: "This is a great idea –
I'll act upon it pronto;
And so I'm off to see the Prof
Researching in Toronto."

He went to J.J.R. Macleod
And said his plan of action
Was now to take some dogs and make
A pancreas extraction.

Macleod approved the new research
And so it came to pass
That many a pup must render up
Its canine pancreas.

"The cure is ready," Banting said,
"Let's call it Insulin.
And now get set, it's time to let
The human trials begin."

The first to have the treatment
Was a boy of just fourteen.
It wasn't long till he grew strong
And great success was seen.

The whole world's press was quick to praise
The four-man team's success.
Soon Banting's name gained lots of fame –
The others, somewhat less.

A knighthood, then the Nobel Prize
Made Frederick Banting proud,
Though he was mad because he had
To share it with Macleod.

He did give half the cash to Best –
Macleod with Collip shared.
So all the four could feel the score
Had justly been declared.

Canadian research had now
A world-wide reputation,
And Banting's name at length became
A credit to his nation.

JOHN DIEFENBAKER
(1895 – 1979)

*(John Diefenbaker spent his childhood in Ontario and in the
North West Territories, and came to Saskatchewan with his family
at the age of fifteen. He became a successful lawyer there, but
always had political ambitions. He eventually won a federal seat,
and went on to lead the Progressive Conservatives to power
with the biggest majority in Canada's history.)*

John's mother asked him, as she eyed
Her little boy with loving pride:
"What do you think you'd like to be?"
"I'll be Prime Minister," said he.

Though he'd achieve his goal, he knew it,
It took him sixty years to do it.
He'd many failures when he ran
For office in Saskatchewan,
But finally he got selected
And was, surprisingly, elected.
For though the Tories had to meet
In 1940, mass defeat,
John Diefenbaker won a seat.

Later, his sixtieth birthday past,
He won the leadership at last
And dealt the Liberals a blow
In two elections in a row.

Fiercely he tore his foes asunder:
His oratory rolled out like thunder
And with his great charisma, Dief
Deserved his title as The Chief.

And yet some critics would insist:
"He's just a Prairie Populist –
His words are humbug and flapdoodle,
The pompous prattle of a noodle!"

Dief promised Canada would see
A rendezvous with destiny.
A noble vision he set forth,
A great new Canada of the North!
Some wondered, though it sounded grand,
Where else he could locate the land?

Justice it's true made many a gain
During John Diefenbaker's reign.
He stopped the harsh discrimination
In quotas set for immigration.

Votes came for each First Nation race
And their first Senator took his place.
Dief was the first P.M. to set
A woman in the Cabinet,
And boldly too he set his sights
On a Canadian Bill of Rights.

And yet, in many people's eyes,
The Chief in power was a surprise.
Though Liberals' control had withered,
John Diefenbaker flapped and dithered.

The Arrow jet which could provide
A symbol of Canadian pride
Was scrapped by Dief because of cost
And fourteen thousand jobs were lost.

The planes were junked, though rumours say
One was kept hidden to this day,
And flies in secret once a year.
Not very credible, we fear:
The rumours also claim it's clear,
In tales as fanciful as Chaucer's,
The factory also made flying saucers!

Dief clashed with Kennedy, made it known
He wanted a non-nuclear zone,
Bought U.S. planes which stayed unused

When nuclear warheads he refused.
By Cuba too he was confused,
And Kennedy was most derisive
When Dief's response was indecisive.

Financially he could be blind:
The Governor of the Bank resigned,
And Dief would make the nation holler
When he devalued Canada's dollar.

Then Parliament, the outlook grim,
Voted No Confidence in him.
John had achieved his boyhood mission
But now he leads the Opposition.
His lurid language he parades
In fierce and furious tirades.

Into his eighties he would be
A fervent federal M.P.,
Attracting with advancing age
Warmth and respect instead of rage:
John Diefenbaker now with pleasure
Had turned into a national treasure!

CHARLOTTE WHITTON
(1896 – 1975)

*(Charlotte Whitton was a brilliant student at Queen's University,
and went on to become a pioneer reformer in social work
and child welfare. She campaigned for women's rights and when
she went into politics in Ottawa, she became the first woman
mayor in Canada's history – a role she played with feisty
and often controversial dedication.)*

Much praise and much abuse was written
About the fiery Charlotte Whitton.
She was indeed a feminist,
Although the term did not exist
When Charlotte first began her fights
To gain for women equal rights.

"We are a power," she said with pride
"Which up till now has been untried.
Women are only rated when
Achieving twice as much as men –
But luckily it's also true,
That isn't very hard to do!"

Our social workers, she maintained,
Should be professionally trained;

For children's welfare, now neglected,
A better deal should be expected.

She told her colleagues: "Try to chase
Each shocking, stark and lurid case.
Only such stories, publicized,
Will get the public galvanized."

Her rage was savage when she went
To fight Alberta's government.
"Unmarried mothers have no option,"
She said, "but settling for adoption.
Alberta gets kids off its hands
By sending them to foreign lands.
They've done it now for quite a time:
Bootlegging Babies, that's their crime!"

Alberta took a libel suit
But Charlotte didn't give a hoot.
The judges trying it, she knew,
Would find her claims were largely true.

Now Charlotte Whitton felt the call
To seek a place in city hall.
Her campaign skillfully she steered:
Hundreds of women volunteered
To help her to achieve her goal,
And Charlotte duly topped the poll.

Soon she was asked to take the chair
As Canada's first woman mayor;
And now her male Controllers' Board
Trembled as Charlotte raged and roared.
Her style was raucous and ferocious –
Her language could be quite atrocious,
And yet for all her ranting noise
She knew her board as "My Dear Boys".

But woe betide a Boy who'd dare
To say one word against the Mayor.
Total respect they must accord her
Or risk being ruled out of order.
She'd threaten, if they didn't cease,
Even to go and call the police.

Once, she forsook her mayoral chair
And to the gallery climbed the stair,
Then heckled her Dear Boys from there.

But Charlotte could be stern and gritty
Defending her beloved city.
She fought against commercial greed
And made the federal rulers heed
The planning laws which they'd abused,
And pay for buildings which they used.

One journal called her and her band
The best free circus in the land.
If so, they could have also written,
The ringmaster was Charlotte Whitton.

She cracked the whip with regularity,
And seemed to gain in popularity.
Maybe her Dear Boys felt dejected,
But four times she was re-elected.
She might be showy, fierce and loud,
But Charlotte made her city proud.

NORMA SHEARER
(1900 – 1983)

(Norma Shearer grew up in Montreal, and from there her mother brought her to New York and then to Hollywood, to get her into films. She became a star, and married the movie mogul Irving Thalberg, one of the bosses of M.G.M.)

At the age of just fourteen
Young Norma was a beauty queen
And then a popular child model;
Her mother said: "This is a doddle!
Destined for fame you surely are –
You're going to be a movie star!"

So in New York they went to town –
The Ziegfeld Follies turned her down
And so an extra she became
And had some bit parts to her name.

Then a tycoon in Hollywood
Said; "This girl could be really good."
Now Irving Thalberg was the man
Who first became a Shearer fan.
He'd soon become a powerful player -
A boss of Metro-Goldwyn-Mayer.

To California she'd go
To screen-test at the studio.
On first seeing Thalberg, quite unwary,
She thought he was a secretary –
For even in those early days
Norma had hoity-toity ways.

Her screen-test chance she nearly lost:
One of her eyes was slightly crossed
And a producer also chose
To comment on her bumpy nose.

So Louis Mayer then said No.
Her face all wet with tears of woe
She pleaded for another go.

Mayer relented – one small part
At least would give the girl a start;
And in the rushes he detected
A quality he'd not expected:
She looked intense, still and demure,
And unlike some stars, even pure!

Now launched upon the movie scene
In those days of the silent screen,
Her repertoire of parts grew wider:
She even played a bareback rider.

Thalberg was always there beside her
To choose her roles and groom and guide her.

Soon, there were roses and romance,
And many a night they'd dine and dance.
The *Yes Sir! That's My Baby* tune
Was making Norma Shearer swoon,
But they were rarely quite alone:
Her mother came, as chaperone.
That is perhaps why Irving chose
To speed the courtship, and propose.

Their wedding, lavish, loud and glittering,
Had all the gossip columns twittering.
The gossips said, with deadly charm:
"This will do her career no harm!"

Norma indeed achieved her goal
And played in many a starring role.
She was endearingly petite
At just one inch above five feet.
She made the audiences love her
While leading men all towered above her.

Laughton and Tyrone Power were two;
The first moustache Clark Gable grew
Was for a film with Norma Shearer
And brought his super-stardom nearer.

She won an Oscar, and would get
Star roles in *Marie Antoinette*
And *Romeo and Juliet*.

But while the fans she was bewitching
The other female stars were bitching.
She made Joan Crawford very cross –
Joan said: "You're never at a loss
When you are sleeping with the boss!"

Her enmity was unremitting:
For Norma's close-ups, Joan was sitting
Blithely beside the camera, knitting.

Her rivals Norma would condemn:
She was the Queen of M.G.M.
And Norma Shearer wasn't kidding
When telling staff to do her bidding.

She sent for stylish clothes one day
And ordered Wardrobe staff to stay
And spend all night, with much impatience,
To make a set of imitations.
She sent the originals, what's more,
Right back, unpaid for, to the store.

At 37, Thalberg died,
And vainly Norma Shearer tried

To keep her queenly status still.
There were disputes about the will,
And Louis Mayer soon would show
That he could be a ruthless foe.

Then Norma wed her ski instructor
Who from her widow's status plucked her,
And Norma left the movie scene.
But still remembered she has been.
Websites and memorabilia are
Constant reminders of the star
Who left Quebec to find she could
Become a Queen in Hollywood.

GRANT McCONACHIE
(1909 – 1965)

(Known as one of the fathers of Canadian aviation,
Grant McConachie grew up in Edmonton and was one of the
pioneer bush pilots who opened up the Canadian North.
He survived several crashes and went on to become President of
Canadian Pacific Airlines – CPA – which first linked Canada with
Asia and Australia. He believed fervently that Canada should be
among the world leaders in the development of modern aviation.)

An airline pioneer was Grant McConachie,
He was like a battling businessman with wings.
If the world of aviation had a monarchy
Then he could claim to be among the kings.

He learned his flying while he was a student
In a club where makeshift aircraft
Made their flights.
Such travel many thought was hardly prudent
And were not surprised
The pilots called them 'Kites'.

With two old planes he started up a business –
To be a bold bush pilot was his wish.
He swooped and dived

With not a trace of dizziness
Transporting produce, prospectors, and fish.

He did some thrill rides
With the Brothers Ringling
In a carnival which through the prairies played.
The passengers could feel their hearts a-tingling –
They paid a cent for every pound they weighed.

Those days inspired Grant's talent for promotion
And he used it when he ran the CPA,
Creating routes that spanned the land and ocean
And travelled by the Arctic Circle way.

Before the rest, jet aircraft he was buying,
A prospect of the future in his gaze –
He remembered those old planes that he was flying
When Edmonton to Whitehorse took five days.

He foresaw that jet-age airports would be needed
And wanted Canada to lead the way;
And no one had the sort of vision he did
Of the vital role that tourism would play.

He passionately favoured competition
When monopolies and mergers were in sight,
And scorned the views of those in opposition,
For he somehow knew that he was always right!

He gazed upon the future without blinking
Determined it was going to go his way –
And we wonder just what thoughts
He might be thinking
Of the aviation industry today...

MARGARET LAURENCE
(1926 – 1987)

(Margaret Laurence was born in Neepawa, Manitoba.
Her mother and father both died before she was ten,
and she was brought up by her aunt and grandfather.
From her childhood years she always wanted to be a writer,
and after going to university in Winnipeg, she married
Jack Laurence, a civil engineer, and lived abroad and in Vancouver
and Ontario, becoming Canada's most successful novelist.)

In Neepawa, Manitoba,
Margaret Laurence as a child
With the loss of both her parents
Never could be reconciled.

Through her life, although she hid it,
She was often insecure.
Writing gave her strength and purpose –
Of her talent she was sure.

Like her character Vanessa,
Maybe Margaret's childhood style
Featured pioneering epics
And romance beside the Nile.

From
Mogadishu
to
Manitoba...

LAURENCE of
MANAWAKA

When she went to university
It could surely be no crime
Reading novels in the bookstore
Just one chapter at a time.

Margaret was then beginning
On her own career in fiction.
"Writing" she declared with gusto,
"Is my permanent addiction!"

With Jack, the engineer she married,
She went travelling abroad.
In the Gold Coast and Somalia
Her imagination soared.

Africa, with all its richness,
As a setting served her well
In her books like *This Side Jordan*
And *The Prophet's Camel Bell*.

But her homeland was the setting
For the books that brought her fame,
And the town of Manawaka
Has become a household name.

There the battling Hagar Shipley,
Over ninety years of age,

Triumphing in male society,
Springs to life on every page.

There too, Rachel was a teacher:
A Jest of God a film became,
And her stories of Vanessa
Add to Manawaka's fame.

Margaret Laurence was outspoken
On the issues of the day,
And on race, or nuclear weapons,
She would loudly have her say.

Issues too of sexuality
Books like *The Diviners* spanned.
There were some who, in Ontario,
Would have liked to see it banned.

Others, though, were more perceptive:
With them, *The Diviners* scored.
The Governor General also praised it
And he gave her his Award.

Colleges and universities
Gave her many an accolade,
And the nation saw her portrait
On a postage stamp displayed.

TIM HORTON
(1930 – 1974)

(The founder of the famous chain of Tim Hortons coffee shops was born in Cochrane, Ontario, and grew up to be a hockey star with a place in the Hall of Fame. He played 24 seasons in the NHL, mainly with the Toronto Maple Leafs. The first Tim Hortons store opened in Hamilton, Ontario, in 1964, and the chain was already well established by the time of his death in a car crash ten years later.)

The Stanley Cup four times
Tim's team would claim,
And now a coffee cup maintains his fame.
The man whose name
Has helped the chain to thrive
Began playing hockey at the age of five.

At nineteen, pro games put him to the test:
The Pittsburgh Hornets took him to their nest;
And soon the Maple Leafs recruited Tim –
For eighteen years his star would never dim.

As a defenceman he was like a wall:
With body checks, opponents he would stall;
And Gordie Howe, a big Tim Horton fan,
Declared that he was Hockey's Strongest Man.

Now Tim, who had a family to support,
Wanted more income than he got from sport.
He said: "Hamburger restaurants, I guess,
Could be a recipe for great success."

They weren't, but Tim just wasn't going to stop:
Instead, he started up a doughnut shop.
In Hamilton, in 1964,
The first Tim Hortons opened up its door.

He put an ad into the press, to test
If someone else was ready to invest.
A Hamilton police constable, Ron Joyce,
Thought this would be a wise commercial choice.

So that was how the Hortons chain began:
Soon the Canadian nation it would span.
The route to being an icon Tim had taken,
Like maple syrup or Canadian bacon.
In those first days when ready cash was shorter,
A coffee and a doughnut cost a quarter.

The chain expanded,
And with business brilliance
It soon would count its revenue in millions.
Each eager patron, sipping coffee, savours
Doughnuts which have a dazzling range of flavours.

Tim with a light touch – though a heavy hitter –
Devised the Dutchie and the Apple Fritter.
In hockey too he showed imagination:
Some say the slap shot was his own creation.

Tim lived to see his chain of stores expand,
Spreading their cheery image through the land.
"Always Fresh" became their chosen motto.
One fervent fan compared them to a grotto,
A holy place where worshippers could boast
That they consumed a Timbit like the Host.

The chain's success, like everything commercial,
Attracted comments that were controversial.
Some said the freshness claim was over-stated,
And frozen doughnuts were resuscitated.
The firm was somewhat cagey in reply,
And said that "Always Fresh" did still apply.

There was another rumour to deny:
That in Tim Hortons' thriving doughnut trade,
The Timbit came from where the hole was made!

Today, although the firm has merged with Wendy's,
It still attracts traditionalists and trendies,
To whom Tim Hortons keeps with resolution
Its role as a Canadian institution,
And honours proudly this great player's name,
Just like his place in Hockey's Hall of Fame.

WILLIAM SHATNER
(born 1931)

(Born in Montreal, William Shatner started his acting career in the theatre and in films. Then he landed the television role of Captain Kirk in the Star Trek *series, which made him an international – indeed an inter-galactic – star.)*

Captain James Tiberius Kirk
Gave William Shatner years of work.
An actor really could do worse
Than flit around the universe
To distant worlds and alien skies
Upon the starship *Enterprise*,
Exchanging quips with Mr Spock
And planning where the ship will dock.

It all began in Montreal
Where William heard the theatre's call.
He played Tom Sawyer, we are told,
When he was only twelve years old,
Read Economics at McGill
And in revues revealed his skill.

Stratford, then Broadway, came along –
There was *The World of Suzie Wong*

And even Marlowe's *Tamburlaine*,
Then movies like *The Devil's Rain*.

And then at last the big break came,
The role that really made his name.
He reaped much fame and much reward
When Captain Kirk cried: "All aboard!"
And out among the stars did soar
To Where No Man Had Gone Before.

The *Star Trek* series was a smash
And William Shatner cut a dash
For there was truly no man better
To fill a figure-hugging sweater.

With calming voice and smiling face
He zoomed about in outer space,
And in that inter-stellar trawl
He was the greatest star of all!

Millions of viewers felt they knew
The gallant Captain and his crew:
Doctor McCoy, so skilled and practical
At curing illnesses galactical.

The Captain needed in a crisis
The ship's ingenious devices,

And when a problem got too knotty
"Now beam me up!" he'd order Scotty.

Strangest of all, from Vulcan came
Their colleague, Mr Spock by name,
With ears that pointed at the ceiling.
He was devoid of any feeling
Or passions of the kind that warm us
And yet his brain was quite enormous.

Their starship waged relentless war
On hostile aliens galore.
The Klingons after many chases
Snarled with their corrugated faces
As Kirk confirmed, through storm and strife
The virtues of our way of life.

Now William Shatner, just like Kirk,
Found diets do not always work:
His waist, you'd notice when he's standing,
Is, like the Universe, expanding.

But still the *Star Trek* fans exult –
The fantasy becomes a cult,
And Trekkies meet to shout and cheer
Whenever Kirk or Spock appear.

When William Shatner's on parade
He always gets an accolade.
The greatest compliment is paid
When spoofs and parodies are made.

Web-sites display, without apology,
The First High Church of Shatnerology,
While others tell us, tongue-in-cheek,
The language known as Shatner-Speak.
And William Shatner joins the fun
In shows like *Third Rock from the Sun*.

Though many other shows he'd do –
Films and TV, an album too –
Nothing can ever quite eclipse
The memory of those *Star Trek* trips.
Round William there will always lurk
The sturdy form of Captain Kirk
Who swore throughout the firmament
To boldly go – and boldly went!

ALICE MUNRO
(born 1931)

(Alice Munro was born and grew up in rural Ontario where many of her stories are set. She was 37 when her first collection of short stories was published, and she went on to become one of Canada's most celebrated writers, winning world-wide recognition and many awards.)

From Dawson City to distant Dallas
Readers all relish the works of Alice.
"When I grew up in Ontario
I never expected such fame to know,"
　　Says Alice.

When she went to work as a servant girl
　Toronto life was no social whirl:
"Servants aren't thought to have eyes and ears
So one learns a lot from the things one hears,"
　　Said Alice.

She married and then to Victoria came –
Now Munro's bookstore's a famous name.
Her three young daughters were her delight –
"Short stories were all I found time to write,"
　　Said Alice.

Her settings are towns, remote and small:
"You get no privacy there at all,
And other people decide your role –
To reveal such lives is a writer's goal,"
    Said Alice.

With vivid details her tales are rife:
A gesture, a glance, brings a world to life.
In bleak old age or in anxious youth
Her characters each get their moment of truth
    From Alice.

The first of her critical accolades
Came for her *Dance of the Happy Shades*.
The Governor General to this accords
The first of several such Awards
    To Alice.

So the prizes come and the critics applaud
For Alice Munro, at home and abroad.
Her country's prestige she has helped to raise
But the greatest reward is her readers' praise
    For Alice.

FERGIE JENKINS
(Born 1943)

*(Fergie Jenkins was born in Chatham, Ontario, and grew up
playing hockey before switching to baseball as a pitcher.
In his spectacular career, mainly with the Chicago Cubs and the Texas
Rangers, he won 20 games a year, six years in a row.
Altogether he won 284 games, and became the first Canadian to be
elected to the Baseball Hall of Fame in Cooperstown, New York.)*

*(These verses are set to the tune of the celebrated baseball song,
"Take Me Out to the Ball Game.")*

Take me out to the ball game
Take me out with the crowd.
Pitchers a-plenty are walking tall –
Fergie Jenkins was king of them all.

So we're cheer, cheer, cheering for Fergie,
Near three hundred wins to his name,
And with one, two, three strikes they were out
At the old ball game.

He's the star of the ball game
How he pleases the crowd.
There in Chicago he cast his spell
And in Texas they thought he was swell

How they'd cheer, cheer, cheer Fergie Jenkins,
Canada's great baseball name.
Now it's one, two, three and he's there
In the Hall of Fame!

DAN AYKROYD
(Born 1952)

*(Dan Aykroyd was born in Ottawa, and studied Criminology
at Carleton University before deciding on an acting career.
He began on stage with the* Second City *company, moved to
television as a star of* Saturday Night Live, *then on to a movie
career as actor and writer on more than fifty films.)*

At Carleton, studying things criminal,
Dan found the laughter content minimal –
And so he thought he'd make a shift
To exercise his comic gift.

He joined Toronto's *Second City*
In shows satirical and witty.
Delighted audiences flocked
To see the proud and pompous mocked.
(Some thought the group's name was the worst:
Surely Toronto should be First?!)

And then came television fame:
Saturday Night Live made his name.
A founder member of the cast,
Dan now, though thirty years have passed,

Rock on!
Dan Aykroyd
aka Elwood
aka Beldar
aka Doctor
Stantz
etc...

Still pops up there with regularity
In scenes of humour and hilarity.
And then, perhaps what pleased him most,
He finally became its host.

With John Belushi as a friend
On and off screen, good times he'd spend.
Blues Brothers, with its car-chase stunts
Caused the producers more than once
To wince at costs – Dan could exult:
The movie has become a cult.

And there were further hectic chases
With Eddie Murphy, *Trading Places*.
Driving Miss Daisy also came
To bring its actors great acclaim.
For Dan, as well as acclamation,
It brought an Oscar nomination.

In many movies, he's appeared
With creatures creepy, crazed and weird.
In *Ghostbusters*, as Doctor Stantz,
The monsters never stood a chance.
The *Alien Stepmother* was hell
And *Coneheads* cast an ugly spell.

Some films Dan Aykroyd wrote as well:
The cops who often feature there

Reflect an interest he can share:
He sometimes offers for inspection
His cherished police-force badge collection.

He goes in squad cars with the force
And rides a policeman's bike, of course.
And he can boast an added bounty:
A grandfather who was a Mountie.

His forebears also liked to nurture
A role as psychical researcher.
Dan made this fascination formal:
His series on the paranormal
Showed off a new side of the actor –
They called the television show *Psi Factor*.

Dan Aykroyd there has been the host
To many a tale of ghoul and ghost,
Poltergeist probes and eerie jaunts
To spooky supernatural haunts.
Viewers were always entertained
By stories of the Unexplained.

No mystery shrouds Dan's success –
His talent got him there, no less.
To us he need make no apology
That he abandoned Criminology.

JULIE PAYETTE
(Born 1963)

(Julie Payette was born in Montreal and studied engineering and computer science at McGill and Toronto universities. In 1992 she was selected for astronaut training by the Canadian Space Agency. She joined the crew of the space shuttle Discovery *which travelled to the International Space Station in 1999.)*

When Julie was young you can bet
Her sights on high flying were set.
As a child she would follow
The flights of Apollo
Saying: "I'll be an astronaut yet!"

The attraction of space was hypnotic
Her research refined and exotic
On machines you can teach
To recognize speech
And arms whose controls are robotic.

She believes you should have versatility –
She runs, skis and swims with agility;
Her piano inspires
And she sings with top choirs
And has wide multilingual ability.

When Canada's space-planners met
New astronaut trainees to vet,
Of five thousand and more
They selected just four
And among them was Julie Payette.

SHANIA TWAIN
(Born 1965)

*(Shania Twain grew up in poor circumstances in
Timmins, Ontario, and even as a child she sang in clubs and bars.
She continued in the music business and hit the real big time when
she met and married record producer Mutt Lange. She is now the
biggest selling female solo artist in the world, packing in the
crowds at huge stadiums everywhere.)*

From Timbuctoo to Tallahassee
Fans in millions hold her dear:
The lassie with the sassy chassis,
Bubbling with relentless cheer.

You'd have to be a Jeremiah
Not to warm to sweet Shania.

Her mother scorned the warning not to
Put your daughter on the stage,
Told Shania she had got to
Go out there and earn a wage.

Clubs and bars became her scene
Long before she turned thirteen.

Nashville then had all the action –
She sang country for a while;
Then she fell for Mutt's attraction –
Rock and roll was more his style.

Mutt's talents quite belied his name
And took them both to wealth and fame.

Songs both glad and melancholic
She and Mutt spend months creating.
A life some say is workaholic
They would call exhilarating.

And she has no cause to wonder:
"Whose bed have your boots been under?"

Once she went for tomboy dressing –
Now it's often silver boots,
Hotpants, veils her form caressing,
Leopard-spotted trouser suits.

Critics call her act robotic
And mechanically erotic.

Critics – fans would like to flatten 'em,
Forever and For Always loyal.

Albums all go multi-platinum
And they treat her like a royal.

Nothing her career can scupper –
She's *UP, UP, UP,* and going UPPER!

AUTHOR'S NOTE

I was delighted to be asked by our publisher, that Fabulous Canadian Kim McArthur, to collaborate with my friend Aislin on another volume celebrating the achievements of Canadians past and present. The characters in our new collection come from the worlds of medicine, sport, politics, art, literature, espionage, bootlegging and science fiction – and the Canada Goose makes a welcome appearance too.

I want to thank the Canadian Embassy in Dublin and the London Library for their help with my research, and also Marsha Boulton for her lively series of *Just a Minute* biographies, and Margaret Horsfield for her fascinating biography of Cougar Annie.

Aislin has created another gallery of wonderfully funny and perceptive portraits, and Mary Hughson has designed the book with elegant skill. Kim McArthur's dynamic enthusiasm has, as ever, been an inspiration to us all.

Gordon Snell

CARTOONIST'S NOTE

"It's an odd job, making decent people laugh." – Molière

And, to that end, I would like to express my appreciation to my partner in this ever-growing series of books, Gordon Snell. His clever, dashing takes on all things Canadian are a joy to illustrate.

Thanks also to my wife, Mary Hughson, for her expertise, knowledge and patience. Let me mention that none of this would ever get finished without the bubbling enthusiasm of all the gang at McArthur and Company.

Finally, as always, I must mention the on-going support of two indispensible individuals here at The Gazette in Montreal: Gaëtan Côté and Pat Duggan.

Terry Mosher (Aislin)